QUICK START GUIDE

for Network Marketing

*Get Started FAST,
Rejection-FREE!*

KEITH & TOM "BIG AL" SCHREITER

Published by Fortune Network Publishing
PO Box 890084
Houston, TX 77289 USA

Telephone: +1 (281) 280-9800

BigAlBooks.com

ISBN-13: 978-1-948197-17-5

ISBN-10: 1-948197-17-0

Contents

PREFACE

We hear the motivational speech by the big leader: "I started slow, but over time I learned what to say and do, and then my business grew faster."

Well, that makes sense. When we learn to do things better and then faster, our business succeeds.

But why not learn how to do our business better and faster now?

Why wait?

This is not the time for patience and endless persistence. We want action and growth in our business now. Why not do the things that will cause our businesses to grow immediately?

This book shows us high-quality shortcuts and techniques that grow our business fast ... now. We will talk about what to say not only to our prospects, but what to say to ourselves. Yes, sometimes the programs inside our heads slow us down in the beginning.

If we are brand-new, or even an old pro at network marketing, these techniques can make us better now.

Let's get started.

BIG AL
W O R K S H O P S

I travel the world 240+ days each year.
Let me know if you want me to stop in your
area and conduct a live Big Al training.

→ **BigAlSeminars.com** ←

FREE Big Al Training Audios

Magic Words for Prospecting

plus Free eBook and the Big Al Report!

→ **BigAlBooks.com/free** ←

SHORT IS BETTER THAN LONG.

When talking to our prospects, here is an easy rule to remember. "Short is better than long."

Want proof?

What would happen if we were to ask 100 random people, "Would you like to hear the long story, or the short story?"

What do you think their replies would be? Almost 100% of these random strangers would say, "Please give me the short story."

Why is this? Because people feel pressured for time. They have jobs, messages to answer, television programs to watch, children, hobbies, relationships, and more. They make instant decisions on where they can invest their limited time. And they want us to be quick.

When we meet someone, friend or stranger, they all think the same thing.

- "Will this be interesting?" If it will be interesting, they can afford to spend a few seconds or minutes of their time listening to us.

- "Get to the point." They've decided to spend some of their precious time with us. They don't want it to be wasted!

Pretty brutal. But, this is the reality. People don't have time for all our ideas and agendas. They only have time for themselves.

And they don't even have enough time for themselves, so they feel constant stress.

Want further proof? Try this.

Imagine we get a phone call from a stranger who says, "I just need 30 minutes of your time."

What are we thinking? "Are you crazy? I have a long queue of decisions I am working on right now. I don't have time to hear your sales pitch. I don't even know what this is about. I can't afford to spend any of my precious time with you. 30 minutes? Are you out of your mind? I can't even afford five minutes of phone time to listen to you and your agenda."

This explains why it is difficult to get appointments not only with strangers, but also with friends.

Want even more proof? Try this.

Imagine we are talking to a salesman. We ask a simple question. The answer from the salesman goes on and on. The salesman loves talking about his company's special benefits. Now we get bored. We feel irritated. This is taking too long. Our backlog of things to do is growing.

Got the feeling? Yes, we only want super short answers to our questions when dealing with salespeople.

Bottom line?

There is the "long way" of talking to people that doesn't work.

There is the "short way" of talking to people that does work.

If we want to build our business fast and put it into momentum, here is our plan.

#1. Talk to people ... but keep it short. Prospects love this. This saves us time also. If we want to build our business fast, we can't waste hours with a single prospect. We need to sort prospects out now.

#2. Make sure our limited words count. Yes, we need skilled sequences of words. Random verbal diarrhea and chit-chat are for the amateurs. Professionals use magic words, soundbites, word pictures, and immediate closing techniques.

Want to see the difference this makes?

Let's jump to the next chapter. We want word-for-word examples of the difference between professional words and random verbal diarrhea.

Better, shorter words.

Rather than talk about theory, let's use some real-life examples. Then we can decide if we want to continue amateur random chit-chat, or talk like professionals.

Here are some examples.

Diet products.

Our overweight prospect is typical. He wants to delay his buying decision indefinitely. Not a good thing for us, however, if we want to build fast. Our prospects have a procrastination program. A procrastination program?

Yes. Our prospects made bad decisions in the past. When they made those bad decisions, their subconscious minds thought about those decisions over and over again. This is painful. So the subconscious mind makes a program that says, "Don't you ever make another decision again. It might turn out bad. And then we will feel bad again."

Ouch.

If we have already learned our closing skills, we know how to handle this. But if we are brand-new, we don't know what to do.

Our overweight prospect complains, "That is a lot of money. I need to think about it. I need to research the glycemic index of each of your products." Etc.

What is the amateur response?

"Well, I can assure you that our glycemic indexes are low. Plus we have over 1,000 testimonials already here in our city. Our research scientist can beat up every other research scientist. Because we use quality ingredients, the potency of our products exceeds the industry standard. By following our attached reduced-carbohydrate and exercise plan, you will attain consistent results ..."

Our response just gets worse and worse. But we get the point. This is what amateurs do. We don't know any better when we first get started.

So what do professionals say?

Professionals can't afford to spend time on these peripheral issues. These issues won't move our prospects closer to a decision. Instead, we need to concentrate on the core issue and result. Here is what professionals could say that is shorter and more effective.

"All of your dieting, all of your starving, all of your gym memberships, all of your diet products, and all of your exercise has given you the body you are looking at right now. Would it be okay if we try something that will work?"

Ka-ching!

Done.

In only two sentences, we get to the core issue and the decision.

We don't waste our prospects' time with their petty issues and delays. We get to the point. And our prospects appreciate that. In fact, they love it!

At this moment our prospects have a decision to make. In this example their decision is, "Do I want to continue dieting for the rest of my life and end up looking like I do now? Or, should I try something that works?"

Done.

Electricity service.

Our prospect resists and says, "I don't want to switch my electricity. The current monopoly has always been good to me. And yeah, I could save a little bit of money, but I want to keep my electricity as it is."

How do amateurs reply?

"Oh, but it is safe to change your electricity. We are good people. We can help you save money and our customer service is better. The Deregulation Act of 1993 guarantees that you can always switch back. Many people changed to our service recently and are happy. Let me show you a chart of how much money you could save." Etc.

The amateur distributors go on and on with more benefits, more proof, and more testimonials. Their time investment brings little or no results.

So what do professionals say?

Professionals respect their prospect's insecurity issues. They respect that their prospect has a negative program about change. Rather than argue about these issues, professionals reassure their prospect. They rephrase the offer to their prospect in a way that isn't scary, and then get to the point.

How would that sound?

"Don't change your electricity. That would be silly. Instead, simply have us send you a lower bill."

Now the prospect doesn't fear that someone will mess with his electricity. Who knows what his fears could have been? Maybe he thought someone would drain the old electricity out of his house, and then replace it with lower voltage? Or maybe that if there was a storm, his electricity wouldn't get reconnected?

These fears are now gone. He doesn't have to change his electricity provider. All he has to do is receive a lower bill every month.

Three short, simple sentences. Professionals address this prospect's fears and provide a safe solution. In less than ten seconds, the problem is solved.

Vitamins and nutrition.

Our prospects complain, "All those vitamins and health foods will cost a lot. We don't want to spend that much money. If we took everything we needed for our health, that would cost us over $150 a month!"

How do amateurs reply?

"But these are the very best vitamins ever. Having these extra antioxidants can support your immune system. And everything is organic. Sure it is expensive, but it is all-natural. No additives. I have 13 research reports comparing our vitamins to our competitors' vitamins. Plus, we have a 20-year history of quality manufacturing. You need these vitamins, so would you please buy them?"

Already we can see that this will have a bad ending.

So what do professionals say?

"You can save a lot of money on your vitamins and health foods ... by dying early."

Okay, slightly exaggerated. Only illustrating that we have to get to the point now. We can't engage in mental jujitsu discussions with our prospects. We want our prospects to hear our offer loud and clear. Then, our prospects can decide if our offer will serve them or not. That is all we ask.

We are not in charge of our prospects' decisions. They are. But we are in charge of being direct and clear so our prospects hear and understand what we are offering.

Skincare and makeup.

Our prospect resists and tells us, "Oh, I am fine with whatever I find at the discount store. Sometimes the product fell on the floor, cracked, and only has a little bit of bacteria that I can scrape off the top. I save a lot of money that way. And the powders and the color matching? Well, I do experiment a lot. Sometimes I get bargains at the local flea market. I think I look good most of the time. Occasionally someone might tell me that I look like I graduated from the clown school of makeup. However, that doesn't happen much."

How do amateurs reply?

"A former semi-famous movie star endorsed our makeup line. So you know it has to be good. With over 16,000 colors and shades to choose from, I know I can find the right matching colors for you. Our anti-aging skincare? Sure, there are other anti-aging skincare products out there, but ours will make you look 20 years younger. Of course this means that teenagers can't use it. Do you want to buy?"

This may sound good, but our prospect isn't convinced.

So what do professionals say?

"Yes, our coordinated look will save you time every morning. But that isn't the reason you should buy from us. Your face is your best first impression. You only get one chance at it. We will make you look great every time."

Professionals don't have to address every tiny objection prospects make. They concentrate on the big picture. Professionals make prospects forget their tiny issues and focus on a "yes" or "no" decision.

Travel club.

Our prospect says, "So what do you do?"

Amateurs reply, "We are a cooperative travel connection company that has high-discount contracts with many of the most famous suppliers. We have surety bonds with the IATA and government licensing department, so you know your deposits are safe with us. Our executive team has 141 years of travel experience. We won an award two years ago. Because of our group buying power, we can provide low prices on your next cruise or vacation. I can send you the link to watch our company video."

Our prospect is thinking, "My fault. I asked for a sales pitch."

So what do professionals say?

Professional: "Do you take a family holiday every year?"

Prospect: "Yes. Of course. We always look forward to it."

Professional: "Family memories are important. We want to take the most memorable vacations that we can. But of course, we have to be conscious of our budget."

Prospect: "Yes, memorable and luxurious vacations are expensive. But it sure beats staying at my mother-in-law's apartment for two weeks with her 42 cats."

Professional: "For your memorable and luxurious vacations, would you like to spend a lot less?"

Prospect: "I would love that."

Professional: "I can fix that for you."

Done.

Short and to the point.

Our business opportunity.

Our coworker asks, "So what is new with you?"

Amateurs reply, "I have a ground-floor opportunity with the fastest-growing company ever. It is setting new records as we speak. You can make a six-figure income as we are entering our momentum stage. The company founder walks on water when it is frozen, got good grades in school, and his city voted him the most promising up-and-coming executive in the area. There is nothing like it. No competition. All of your friends will want to join. Come listen to our business opportunity presentation this evening."

Coworker: "So what is the name of the company?"

Amateur: "I can't tell you. You might look it up on the Internet and prejudge."

Coworker: "Well, what do they sell?"

Amateur: "I can't tell you now. You have to listen to the whole story at one time."

Coworker: "Will I have to be a salesman?"

Amateur: "Maybe."

Coworker: "Could you tell me a little bit about it first, before I invest my time?"

Amateur: "No. I can't do that. It is sort of visual. You have to see it for yourself."

Coworker: "So what **can** you tell me?"

Amateur: "It is negative people like you that never take advantage of an opportunity. Are you going to join me and listen to the presentation this evening, or not?"

So what do professionals say?

Coworker: "So what is new with you?"

Professional: "I decided I did not want to work this job for the rest of my life. I plan to do something about it."

Coworker: "That's interesting. I don't think I want to be stuck here in this job for the rest of my life either."

Professional: "I don't like taking risks, so I started my own part-time business. I want to make sure it is successful before I quit my job here."

Coworker: "Good idea. We both have families. Is this something you think I could do also?"

Professional: "It would be fun for us to build our businesses together. Then our families could holiday together. Why not check out this business with me this evening? Then you would have at least one more option for the future."

Coworker: "Sure. What time?"

Same opportunity.

Two different ways to talk to prospects.

Most prospects are neutral ... until they meet us. Our conversations can turn neutral prospects into great prospects, or bad prospects.

Say the right words.

The new distributors say, "We talked to our warm market of family and friends. They all said 'no' to me. Now what?"

The answer? If our family and friends hated what we said, then strangers won't like what we say any better. Finding new prospects to ruin won't solve the problem.

Now, that is cold.

Sometimes brutal honesty is what we need to prompt us to change. If everyone is telling us "no," then we have to change what we say.

Many times, prospects don't say "no" to our opportunity. Instead, they say "no" to how we described our opportunity.

What happens when we continue to describe our opportunity poorly? Well, we build persistence and character, but not much else. Unfortunately, we don't earn bonuses on persistence and character-building traits. We earn bonuses on building a team that sells products and services every month.

My experience.

When I started my network marketing career, I was on fire. Here was my chance to build a huge income for my family. What did I do? I did exactly what they told me to do. I talked to people!

Over the next year and 10 months, I talked to over 1,000 people about the business. And at the end of one year and 10 months, I had no distributors and no retail customers. Everything else was okay. I knew the best roads to the meetings. I had the training memorized. My attitude was top-notch. But no one joined.

Why didn't prospects join?

Well, the economy was bad in my area, the weather was miserable, there wasn't any upline support where I lived. Plus the products were too expensive, people were busy, and through some weird, statistical abnormality, I met over 1,000 unmotivated people in a row who wanted nothing more in their lives.

Really? Was that the problem?

Of course not. The problem was me. I was at the "scene of the crime" every time. At every presentation, there I was, saying the wrong words. The words I chose did not motivate prospects to join.

I always thought I heard my sponsor's advice clearly. I thought he told me, "Go talk to people." But thinking back, maybe he told me, "Go talk to people ... correctly."

Saying the right words is a primary skill in our business. Random oral diarrhea and verbal vomit might keep us active, but we won't have the results to show for it.

Here is how I learned that lesson. After one year and 10 months, I had to find a solution. After listening to all my excuses of why people did not join, someone had this conversation with me:

Someone smarter than me: "So tell me, are other people successful in your area?"

Me: "Yes. It is not fair. They only work a little bit and can build a team. I work hard and get no results."

Someone smarter than me: "Do these successful people have the same weather that you do? The same compensation plan? The same company? The same economy?"

Me: "Yes."

Someone smarter than me: "The only difference between you and the successful people in your business is one thing. They say better words. When they are with the same prospect, they use different words than you do. Figure it out."

The change.

I immediately began listening to what the successful people said. They used different words and different phrases. They spent more time talking about their prospects' problems.

I had spent all of my time talking about the company's features and benefits. I was boring.

Prospects love listening to the successful people. Why? Because the successful people's conversations are all about them, the prospects.

What happened when I changed my words? Magic.

Prospects begin to smile when I talked. I stopped talking about my company's features and benefits. The prospects didn't feel like they were being sold to. When I started listening to my prospects' problems, they felt that I cared. We built a stronger rapport.

The result?

After one year and 10 months of total failure, it only took 60 days to replace my full-time income. Yes, after 60 days I walked into my boss's office and said, "I can't fit you into my schedule any longer."

Now, this is interesting. I didn't talk to any new people. I simply returned to the people who told me "no" originally. By re-describing my business using different words, these prospects said, "Sure. We would like to join."

That is how I learned the lesson that people don't turn us down. They don't turn our company or products down.

What really happens?

They turn down how we present our business to them. By changing our words, we get our message understood by more people.

The bottom line.

Our prospects react to the words we say. Here is an example.

We could say to a prospect, "You have a stupid job. You need to join my network marketing business."

Or, we could say to the same prospect, "Would it be okay if you had one more option for money every month?"

Which set of words will get a better reception? The answer is obvious.

So if everyone is telling us "no" when we present to them, then we have to look at ourselves. We are the common denominator in every presentation. The good news is that we can change what we say and we will get different results.

Changing to better words is 100% within our control.

Let's get our heads right first.

As we saw in the last chapter, better words make a difference. To start fast? Short, direct words work best.

But let's look at one issue before we continue. What is inside our heads?

Many times, our internal programs hold us back from action. We fear approaching people or feeling like a sleazy salesman. Even with the best skills in the world, if we are hesitant to talk to people, we can't start fast.

If we can fix this issue inside our heads, then we will know how to fix it for our new team members.

Of course we can reprogram our minds after months and years of personal development. However, to start fast, we don't have that option.

We can't have negative voices inside of our heads that say, "Oh, those people won't be interested. They might be offended that we approached them. We might get rejected."

To build our business fast, we need to remove these negative voices and programs in our heads.

Let's do that now.

"But I don't want to be a salesman."

Most new distributors have this thought. This viewpoint prevents us from contacting friends, co-workers, and relatives. Calling for appointments is difficult. We fear approaching potential prospects.

Why don't we want to be salespeople?

There are many reasons.

1. We don't want to harass our family and friends to buy things.

2. We don't want our friends to say, "You are using our friendship just so you can make money off me."

3. We hate asking favors from people. That feels sleazy.

4. Salesmen get rejected. That hurts.

How did we get these feelings?

Maybe we saw a movie of an aggressive salesman pushing solutions on reluctant prospects. This salesman used obnoxious closing techniques that would make criminals blush. Well, no one wants to be like that.

Everyone hates rejection. When prospects tell us "no," we feel that the rejection is personal.

We can't let this viewpoint linger in our heads.

This viewpoint will paralyze us. If we don't talk to prospects, we won't have a business.

How do we stop these disempowering thoughts inside our heads?

Arguing with our subconscious mind won't work. Imagine telling ourselves, "This is stupid. Only losers fear selling. Let me chant a few more positive affirmations to myself. My vision board is sending me positive vibes. Only weak people have these fears."

That is what we would want our minds to be thinking, but that is a big stretch from our current feelings. We want to be logical, but emotions crush logic every day.

Another logical script we tell ourselves is, "Everyone is a salesman. I sold the boss on hiring me for this job. How did I ever get a date? Or get married? I sell every day!"

Sounds good, but again our subconscious mind's feelings hold strong. Instead of arguing with our subconscious mind, let's create a new belief to replace our fear of selling.

Options!

Here is the message we can tell ourselves to replace our fear of selling. We say, "Don't sell. All we do is offer prospects one more option for their lives."

Now, isn't that what we really do?

Prospects have the option to continue with their lives just as they are. Prospects don't have to listen to us or take our solutions. All we do is offer them one more option. When we look at our business from this viewpoint, we don't feel like a salesperson.

So, no selling, no harassing, no pressuring, no asking favors.

Most prospects welcome the opportunity to have one more option in their lives. Here is an example.

If some of our prospects felt tired, we could offer them a cup of coffee. Now, they have one more choice to solve their problem. We don't sell them the cup of coffee, we don't tell them where we grew the coffee beans. We let them know that coffee could help.

We wouldn't emotionally attach ourselves to the outcome. Our prospects can choose the cup of coffee, or not. If our prospects do not want the coffee, we don't jump off a cliff.

Here's another example.

We take our family to the local restaurant for dinner. Two appetizers, extra bread and a massive entree. We're so full that we can't breathe. At the end of our meal our waitress asks, "Would you like some dessert?"

We smile and reply, "No thank you. Not tonight."

Does our waitress get frustrated that we didn't want dessert?

Does she complain to her manager that nobody wants dessert?

Does she give up on her entire waitressing career because dessert is impossible to sell?

Does she wonder if the price of dessert is too high, even though we didn't ask?

Will she complain to her fellow coworkers that this dessert thing is a pyramid scheme?

No. She offered us the dessert option, and we didn't take it.

No drama. No stress. The world will continue to spin.

Reality check.

Our encounters with prospects are not win-lose, live-or-die situations. Instead, we politely give prospects one more option for their lives.

When we approach prospects with this viewpoint, there is no more rejection. No more fear. No more sleazy salesman feelings. Instead, we feel obligated to talk to our prospects. We don't want to feel as if we are withholding options from their lives.

Think about our family and friends. Some may want an extra income in their lives, some may not. We should not make up their minds for them.

We notify them that an extra income option exists. If they want to know more, they can have a conversation with us. And if they don't want to know more, everything will remain the same in their lives.

This belief makes it easier to approach people.

Want some examples? Our new belief of adding one more option to other people's lives could sound like this. To our brother-in-law, we could say:

"I know you hate your job as much as I do. Tonight, there is a business meeting on how to start our own part-time business. Come with me. At least you will have one more option to consider, instead of working at that job you hate for the rest of your life."

Or, we could say this.

"You and I don't want to work at our jobs for the rest of our lives. My friend, John, has an escape plan. Let's have a cup of coffee with John, listen to him explain his escape plan, and at least we will have one more option to consider instead of suffering at our jobs until we are 70."

Or, we could say this.

"Hey Uncle Joe. I started my own part-time business last month. Let me tell you about it over lunch next week. It might be an option that can help you retire early."

With these approaches, our invitations won't scare our prospects. We don't scream, "Buy! Join!" We simply add one more option to our prospects' lives.

Reinforcing this new belief.

We can continue our self-talk conversation by adding this phrase:

"Our prospects can take our option today, tomorrow, sometime in the future, or never."

This tells our subconscious minds that it is okay for prospects not to take our option immediately. It is okay for prospects **not** to say "yes" to our option.

When it is not the right time for a prospect, we don't take this as a personal rejection. We don't know what is influencing that prospect's decisions.

Our option might never be the right solution for a particular prospect. So, if this prospect never takes our option, it isn't a personal rejection.

Our option will never be a 100% solution for 100% of our prospects 100% of the time.

One more sentence to add a bit of courage.

We continue by telling ourselves, "And prospects love getting extra options in their lives."

This is true, isn't it? Everyone loves having more options to choose from. We wouldn't go to a restaurant that had only one item on their menu. We love choices.

We want our mindset to be, "Prospects will love me for giving them extra options. I feel good about talking to new prospects."

Let's put this all together.

The complete self-talk script goes like this:

"Don't sell. All we do is offer prospects one more option for their lives. Our prospects can take our option today, tomorrow, sometime in the future, or never. And prospects love getting extra options in their lives."

We can't move forward fast if fear paralyzes us from making new contacts. Let's use this script to reprogram our subconscious minds. We are giving one more option to our prospects.

FEEL BETTER ABOUT APPROACHING PROSPECTS?

Great. Now let's get back to using direct, professional language to build quickly.

Most challenges in our business are recurring. These challenges won't go away. We will face them for the rest of our careers ... unless we fix them now. We don't want to be amateur distributors who spend all of our time fighting these challenges.

Some examples?

I'm sure we've all heard, "The products are too expensive."

Will we hear it again? Yes. Now, if we don't know how to answer this objection, this challenge will haunt us for the rest of our careers. We secretly hope our prospects never bring it up. Why not fix this challenge now?

Again, I'm sure we've all heard, "I don't have any money to join."

Will we hear it again? Yes. If we don't learn what to say, we will struggle every time our prospects say this. Why not fix it now?

Want more examples?

How about these:

"I don't have any prospects."

"I don't know who to call."

"I don't know what to say to get appointments."

And the list goes on and on.

All prospects will have these objections until we learn how to present our business properly.

So don't look for prospects who don't have these objections. All prospects have these objections. Instead, we need to learn how to present our business in a way that handles these objections.

As professionals, we want to learn how to handle these challenges now, so we never struggle with them in the future.

Let's tackle the most common ones now.

"IT IS TOO EXPENSIVE!"

We want to talk to our best prospects first, but we fear this objection:

"Oh, your product is so expensive. That's too much money. I can buy a competitor's product for a lot less."

If we carry this fear in our heads, what happens? We avoid talking to prospects. And if we get this objection and handle it badly, this fear increases inside of our heads.

Now logically, we could say this to our prospects:

"Our product is high-quality. There is an old saying that you get what you pay for. We have research. Our scientist can beat up your scientist. You can't trust what you buy from others. You can trust me more. We have a proprietary formula. Our product is trademarked, patented, copyrighted, and won an award once. We have 223 testimonials on our website."

Pretty mediocre, right? We have to do better. Let's fix this objection not only when we talk to prospects, but also inside of our heads.

Step #1: Agree with the objection.

The first rule of handling objections? We have to agree. If we don't agree with our prospect, we lose.

For example, our prospect says, "Your product is too expensive." We could reply by saying, "Oh, you are such a loser. This is small money. You are wrong. You don't understand value."

Bad ending.

Okay, this is exaggerated, but telling our prospect that he or she is wrong will kill our chances for sure.

If we disagree with our prospect, what will our prospect be thinking? Our prospect will think, "I have to have more reasons to support my side of the argument."

The human mind can only think about one thing at a time. This means our prospect is not listening to us!

The more we talk, the more our prospect thinks of new things to say to support his position.

Wait, if we are talking, and the other person isn't listening while thinking of what to say next ... well, we aren't being heard. We are saying all the good reasons to support our viewpoint, and nobody is listening. Our prospect is just waiting for us to shut up so he can talk even more. We lose.

Plus, disagreeing is bad manners.

It shows lack of empathy for our prospects' current situations or life experiences. We don't know what happened to our prospects earlier in the day. We don't know what experiences our prospects had with similar products. We completely discount their experiences and that feels offensive.

Well, if we cannot disagree with our prospects, what other option do we have?

Agree.

Empathy is understanding things from our prospects' points of view. Our prospects believe that our price is too high and our product value is too low.

If we can answer this objection for our prospect, then we will eliminate the fear in our heads that holds us back from talking to prospects.

So let's create a ten-second mini-script that solves the price objection from our prospects.

Ten seconds?

Yes, ten seconds is all the time we have.

Okay. That doesn't give us much time. But we are such interesting people, we should get at least ten seconds, right?

So what must we accomplish during these ten seconds?

First, we have to justify our product's value in our prospect's mind. Currently, our prospect doesn't believe our product is worth this much. We can't argue this logically. We have to command our prospect's mind to instantly believe our product's value.

Second, we want to prevent our prospect from going to cheaper competitors' products that may not be as good. We don't want our prospect to have an inferior experience with a cheap product.

Fortunately, ten seconds is a long time for a professional. We can handle these two items quickly and have time to spare.

So what should we say?

When our prospect tells us that our product is too expensive, we will reply:

"Yes, it is expensive. The company wanted to make a cheaper version, but they knew it wouldn't work. And, they didn't want to rip you off."

This is an easy answer to memorize. And it only takes a few seconds.

Let's see what the words do.

"Yes, it is expensive." We agree with our prospect. Our prospect doesn't have to think of any more facts or excuses to support his position. Now his mind is free. And when his mind is free, what can he do? He can listen to us! This is good.

"The company wanted to make a cheaper version." Every company would love to make a cheaper version. If the final product only costs a few pennies, millions more could afford it. But unfortunately, this is impossible. Products cost money to make.

"But, they knew it wouldn't work." Now our prospect is thinking, "A cheaper version of this product would not work as well." To our prospect, our product now has more value. It needs to be this price to work effectively. When our prospect sees competing products that are cheaper, what will our prospect think? "Yes, this is cheaper. But I am sure they had to compromise and cut out a lot of value to get it to this price. It probably won't work for me."

"And they didn't want to rip you off." We don't need to add this, but it is so much fun to say. Why? It makes us feel good about our company. It makes our prospect feel good about our company.

And the next time our prospect sees a cheaper version of the product, he might be thinking, "If I buy this, it probably won't work as well. I will be ripped off."

Bottom line?

These few sentences justify the price to our prospect. And, this script replaces the negative fear in our heads that our product is too expensive. Problem solved.

So here is the script again.

"Yes, it is expensive. The company wanted to make a cheaper version, but they knew it wouldn't work. And they didn't want to rip you off."

Is this the only way to answer the objection about price?

No. But it is simple and easy to teach to our team.

But here is one more way, just for fun.

Try saying this:

"Our product is sort of a treat or luxury. It is like spending money on movie tickets, cigarettes, lottery tickets, or beer. And we all love a little luxury in our lives."

If our prospects spend money on these things, they can afford our product.

"But I don't have any money to join."

Will this objection ever come up in our network marketing business? Yes, over and over. Let's fix it now.

What does it mean when our prospects say they don't have any money to join?

It could mean that our prospects do have the money to join, but they don't see the value in what we presented. Hopefully, we fixed this problem already by learning to talk clearly and directly.

This objection could also mean that money is very tight. They need their current cash flow for more important expenses for the family.

Remember our first rule of handling objections? We have to agree. Unless we agree, our prospects' minds will be closed to whatever we say.

How long do we have to fix this issue in our prospects' minds? About ten seconds. We have to change their stance from, "We can't join," to "Let's figure out how we can get started now."

This shouldn't be hard. We have a full ten seconds. Remember, ten seconds is a long time for professionals who speak clearly.

We have to start with agreement. We will begin with, "Of course you don't have any money." Now our prospects feel that we heard them and agree with them, and there is no need for them to defend their position.

One caution here: we want to say this sincerely. That means we have to watch our tone of voice so it doesn't sound like sarcasm.

Now that we have opened their minds, what should we say? To get prospects to consider new possibilities, we have to make these new possibilities feel familiar. We do this by telling our prospects a fact they already believe. Our prospects will think, "That fact is true. You and I think the same. We can believe this fact and trust you."

We started with a fact by saying, "Of course you don't have any money." We are doing great.

Let's add our second fact. Now we will say, "Of course you don't have any money, that is why I am talking to you now." Our prospects think, "Wow. You **are** talking to us now. That is totally true. And, you have told me two facts in a row. You are a trusted source of information."

Telling prospects two facts in a row almost puts them into a deep hypnotic trance. Our brains are busy and very underpowered. After two facts, a brain thinks, "This source is trustworthy. Let's put my limited brainpower somewhere where it is needed more. I can believe whatever this person says." A bit of oversimplification, but after two facts our prospects consider us a truthful source of information.

But we are not amateurs. We are professionals. Let's tell our prospects three facts in a row. This will make our rapport and trust go even deeper. Now our reply sounds like this: "Of course you don't have any money, that is why am talking to you now. You don't want to be that way for the rest of your life ... without enough money."

Our prospects have an open mind. We delivered three facts that they believe. Our message is getting through to their brains.

But hey, we have a full ten seconds. Let's add another fact just because we can. Now our reply sounds like this: "Of course you don't have any money, that is why I am talking to you now. You don't want to be that way for the rest of your life ... without enough money. So let's sit down now ..."

Our prospects think, "Wow, we are sitting down now. That is four facts in a row. We think the same. Vulcan mind-meld. Joined at the hip. Blood brother and blood sister. Our minds are the same."

This is what we want our prospects to be thinking so that they hear our entire message. Our goal is to deliver our message inside of our prospects' heads. That's it. Once inside their heads, our prospects can decide if our message will serve them or not. But our biggest challenge is getting the message past all of their negativity, their too-good-to-be-true filters, their what's-the-catch feelings, be-careful-of-salespeople programs, etc.

We are doing a great job so far. So let's add our final phrase, now that our prospects' minds are open. Now our reply will sound like this:

"Of course you don't have any money, that is why am talking to you now. You don't want to be that way for the rest of your life ... without enough money. So let's sit down now and figure out a way to get you started."

Our prospects can easily reply, "Yes." They hear our message loud and clear.

Our prospects started from this point of view: "We don't have any money. We can't do this business. We won't join." After saying these words, our prospects have a new point of view: "We don't want to be broke for the rest of our lives. Let's figure out a way to get started now."

There are many ways to get prospects started who have a temporary cash flow problem. They could presell some products, start lining up prospects, sell the lava lamp they've had in their closet for 40 years, have a garage sale, etc. If our prospects have the desire to get started now, we can figure out a way to help them.

The challenge is to get our prospects to change their point of view quickly. Fortunately, for professionals, this isn't hard to do in ten seconds.

But what if my prospects don't have any time?

We are professionals. We can work this out.

If our prospects complain that they don't have any time, we use the same template. We could say:

"Of course you don't have any time. That is why I am talking to you now. You don't want to be that way for the rest of your life, not having any time for your family or for yourself. So let's sit down now and figure out a way to get you started, so that you can have more time in your life."

That wasn't so hard, was it? We can answer a lot of objections with this template. Here is one more example.

Our prospects say, "But we don't know anyone. We don't have anyone to talk to."

We could answer, "Of course you don't know anyone. That is why I am talking to you now. You don't want to be that way for the rest your life with no friends or contacts. So let's sit down now and get you enrolled in our company training, where you will learn how to meet new people and build your business."

In our business, there are only a few common objections that we will hear over and over. Let's learn how to handle these now so that we can build our business fast.

"I DON'T HAVE ANYONE TO TALK TO."

Okay, we were born to orphaned parents, raised by wolves, and moved to a new city where we don't know anyone. Oh, and we are shy. How do we find people to talk to?

Well, finding people to talk to is the easy part. People are everywhere.

The challenge is figuring out a way to talk to people that is effective and rejection-free.

Approaching strangers.

Let's choose a stranger. How about a sales clerk at a small store? We know this person is paid to be polite, so let's approach this clerk and say:

"Excuse me. I am new to this city. Could you do me a favor?"

The clerk automatically responds, "Sure. How can I help?"

Secretly the clerk is thinking, "Well, maybe I can help you. Depends on what kind of favor you are asking. If you want to borrow money from me, of course I will refuse. But if it is an easy favor, I would be happy to help."

So what kind of favor could we ask for?

We will ask for a favor that is easy and won't pressure the person we are talking to. We will ask for a referral.

What happens when we directly ask someone, "Would you be interested in my business?" This forces that person into a "yes" or "no" decision. If the decision is no, we feel rejected. The person we are talking to doesn't feel that good either.

But when we ask for a referral, this gives the person we are talking to some options. The person could:

- Know someone.

- Not know someone.

- Not know someone now, but will think about it.

- Or, be personally interested in what we say.

There is no time pressure. The person we talk to may or may not be able to help us right now. And that is okay.

Why not ask for the perfect referral?

Most people know 200 people that we don't know. We don't want to talk to all 200 of his or her friends. We only want to talk to the most qualified prospects who want to take action now. This will save us a lot of time. We need to start fast.

There is a marketing formula that helps us find people who will take action immediately. Here is the formula:

"I am looking for people who *<have this problem>* and want to fix it."

Prospects worry about their problems. It is easier to motivate prospects to fix problems than to motivate them to reach for our wonderful benefits. We want to locate people with a problem that our products or opportunity can solve.

The last part of the formula, wanting to fix it, narrows our search to prospects who want to take action immediately. Many people have problems but don't want to fix them. These are not our best prospects when we are trying to build our business fast.

Want some examples of people with problems who don't want to fix them?

- An elderly grandparent who says, "No, I don't want any health products. My children visit me more when I pretend to be sick."

- A coworker who says, "Yes, I need more money, but I don't have any time. After I watch my favorite shows at night, I am too tired to think about anything else."

- An overweight person who doesn't want to lose weight.

- A 65-year-old who hasn't started saving for retirement, and doesn't see the need to start now.

There is an old saying, "We can run with 1,000 motivated people, but we can only drag one."

People who don't want to fix their problems will only slow us down. We will respect their decision to stay where they are for now.

Let's put the formula to work.

To the sales clerk, we could say,

"I am looking for people who are bored with their jobs, and are looking for something else."

That was easy. The sales clerk does not feel pressured. And our sales clerk:

1. Knows someone.

2. Doesn't know someone.

3. Can't think of anyone now, but will keep us in mind.

4. Is personally interested.

All four of these outcomes are rejection-free.

Even if our sales clerk doesn't know anyone, our sales clerk is almost apologetic to us.

Now, if someone is recommended to us, what do we know about this person?

1. This person is bored with his current job.

2. This person is looking for options now.

Wow. We are talking to the best prospects now.

Ready for more examples of this formula at work?

Now that we have our formula, let's make sure our words are the best they can be. Again, here is the formula:

"I am looking for people who <have this problem> and want to fix it."

First, let's create some interesting sentences for our business opportunity:

- I am looking for people who hate commuting to work, and would rather work out of their homes.
- I am looking for people who hate their bosses, and would love to be their own boss.
- I am looking for people stressed for time, who would like more time with their family.
- I am looking for people who will retire soon, and would love to double their retirement pension.
- I am looking for mothers with stretch marks who don't want them.
- I am looking for people who have two jobs, but would prefer just one job.
- I am looking for people who want to diet, but can't find the time to exercise.
- I am looking for ladies who love perfume, but hate paying high prices.

What do we know about the prospects who respond? They have this problem, and they want to fix this problem.

Great prospects!

This is an easy pattern.

Let's do more.

- I am looking for people with a lot of credit card debt, who want to pay it off quickly.

- I am looking for people with electric bills who would rather pay a lower rate.

- I am looking for people who want to take vitamins, but can't swallow pills.

- I am looking for single moms who want to change their lives.

- I am looking for people who love coffee, and also want to lose weight.

- I am looking for college graduates with student loans, who want to pay off their loans in three years.

- I am looking for people who are addicted to traveling, and would like to get paid for it.

- I am looking for people who hate their jobs, and would like to have a career helping people.

- I am looking for people who love social media, and want to get paid for their addiction.

- I am looking for people who are underpaid, and want to be paid what they are worth.

- I am looking for busy moms who want a career with flexible hours.

- I am looking for women over 30 who hate wrinkles.

- I am looking for parents who love their children, and want an extra income to put their children into private school.

- I am looking for people who love coffee breaks, and would love a career taking five coffee breaks a day, chatting with new people.

Why does this seem so easy?

Because people are pre-sold. Most people want what we have to offer.

We seldom hear people say:

- "I wish I had less money in the bank."
- "This fat looks good on me. Maybe I should add more."
- "Wow. My wrinkles are getting deeper. I feel like they are giving me character."
- "I hope my electricity bill gets higher soon."
- "If only I could appear older for my high school reunion."
- "I sure hope I can pay full retail price when I shop."
- "Nope. Forget about better holidays for us. My family loves staying at my sister-in-law's apartment with her 32 cats."

We have what our prospects need to solve their problems.

We give our prospects an option to solve their problems.

And then ... we take the volunteers.

Can we use this formula for posting on social media?

Of course. But as we will learn in a later chapter, this won't be nearly as effective as talking directly with prospects. Posting on social media is a low-level communication.

However, if we are awake late at night and scrolling through our social media, why not?

It only takes a minute to post. Nothing wrong with having a little extra prospecting working for us in the background.

And think about who might reply to our posts: only pre-sold prospects who have this problem and want to fix it now.

Finding people to talk to is easy.

People are everywhere. We have an unlimited number of people to talk to. The only reason we thought we had limits was because we didn't know how to talk to people rejection-free.

The secret is not finding people to talk to. The secret is saying the right things when we talk to people.

Using this marketing formula makes it easy to talk to anyone, anywhere. And the best part is that we will be talking to highly-motivated prospects who want to take action now.

As we learn to say the right words, our business gets easier and easier.

Notice how we are talking about our prospects' problems a lot?

Are prospects more interested in solving their problems, or in the awesome benefits of our products and business?

The answer is pretty clear.

The #1 topic that prospects love? Themselves.

When we talk about our prospects, and then talk about their problems, we become the most interesting person in the world.

Why?

Because problems are about our prospects. Benefits are all about us, our products, and our business. Prospects care about themselves, not about us.

"WHO SHOULD I CALL FIRST?"

Now that we have more confidence in our business abilities, who should we call first?

- Should we call the prospects most likely to join?
- Or should we call prospects that are less likely to join?

The answer is obvious. We want to call people who will want to join our business or use our products. The people we already know have some trust and belief in us. Strangers do not.

One of the early steps in the decision-making process is the prospect wondering, "Can I trust you and believe you?" If we don't get past this step, well, we won't go very far. No matter how awesome our offer is, prospects won't join or buy if they don't trust and believe us.

If we are just starting, we haven't yet learned the skills of creating instant rapport with strangers. Without trust and belief, our message will fall on deaf ears.

So let's talk to the people who already know, like, and trust us. They are the people most likely to join us early in our career.

Prospect #1.

Our best friend. Why?

One of the reasons we have a best friend is that we have common interests. If we love our new business, chances are that our best friend will love our business also.

Also, our best friend knows us well. We don't have to create trust and belief. This means that we can skip that step in our conversation.

What can we say to our best friend? Let's try this:

"Hi. I just joined a new business. You are my best friend. I would like us to do this together."

Does that seem straightforward? Sure. It's easy. We are talking to our best friend. We will get better at inviting and setting appointments later.

But for now, let's call our best friend first.

You might be thinking, "Don't I need a sales script to call my best friend?"

No. We get the appointment with our best friend because of our relationship, not because of a slick, manipulative sales script. Plus, don't you think our best friend will be able to tell if we use some impersonal sales script?

Our best friend will feel our passion, belief, and desire to share the good news. And why not? All we do is offer people one more option for their lives.

But what if we feel embarrassed because our last recommendation didn't work out?

Well, we don't want our best friend to be left behind as we build this business. If we withhold our business and keep it secret from our best friend, what kind of friendship is that? Our best friend should at least have a chance to say "yes" or "no" to our opportunity.

Plus, how embarrassing would it be if our best friend found out about the opportunity from someone else?

So yes, call our best friend first and give our best friend the option of joining us in our new business.

This works well when we sponsor someone new. Immediately after enrolling a new distributor, we should say, "Let's call your best friend first."

If needed, we can explain why. However, most new distributors will take our recommendation. It is the easiest way to get the first appointment for our brand-new distributor.

We want to build fast.

Prospect #2.

Who should we call next? Let's ask ourselves this question:

"Of all the people I know, such as friends, relatives, and coworkers, is there at least one person who FEELS the same way that I do? Someone who wants to have a new career or a great part-time income?"

That should give us many more great people to contact.

And why do we concentrate on how someone feels? Because feeling the same way that we do is much stronger than thinking the same way that we do. We want to talk to the easiest and most motivated prospects first.

It is fun to talk to prospects who feel the same way we do. We have the same viewpoint. We have the same motivation. And we will have the same excitement because we can see the potential of our business.

When we are with our new team members, this is an excellent question to ask them, so that they talk to their best prospects first. Here it is again.

"Of all the people you know, such as friends, relatives, and coworkers, is there at least one person who FEELS the same way that you do? Someone who wants to have a new career or a great part-time income?"

We can get their best prospect, their best running buddy, their best friend forever, their most qualified referral by saying this little referral script.

For products?

Here are some quick examples of this referral script:

"Of all the people you know, such as friends, relatives, and coworkers, is there at least one person who FEELS the same way that you do? You know, someone who wants to lose weight, but hates dieting?"

"Of all the people you know, such as friends, relatives, and coworkers, is there at least one person who FEELS the same way that you do? You know, someone who hates paying full retail price and would like to pay less for their electric bill?"

"Of all the people you know, such as friends, relatives, and coworkers, is there at least one person who FEELS the same way that you do? You know, someone who hates wrinkles and is always trying to look younger?"

Some people will give us great referrals, some will not. But we won't get any referrals unless we ask.

Prospect #3 and more.

Let's grab our phone. Our personal contact list is huge.

Let our contacts know one-by-one that we have an extra option for them. That way our conversations or messages are short and rejection-free. Our personal contacts can choose whether they want to know about our option or not.

Our obligation is to let them know that there is an option. We are not obligated to force them to hear the option. That is their choice.

Do we need to have a big list of potential people to contact?

No.

There is an old saying, "It isn't the size of the list. It is the relationships in the list."

A list of three people who FEEL the same way we do will produce better results than a list of 5,000 social media "friends" and low-level contacts.

If our past relationships with people have been transactional, and we didn't become real friends, don't panic. We will meet new people.

But, if we have real friends, let's talk to them first and give them one more option in their lives.

But what if they don't take our option?

Fine. It is only an option. In that case we will ask them if there is anyone they know that would like to take our option. We now know how to do that.

But why should we call our friends and relatives first?

Because we already have rapport. They trust us and believe us. We don't have to spend time establishing rapport. We can get to the point. We can tell them about our business and they will listen with an open mind.

What if I have a mental block?

If we don't want to call our friends first, we have to ask ourselves why. Here are two obvious reasons.

#1. We don't fully believe in our business. We don't feel that we offer a great product or opportunity. We don't want our friends to fail. Because we aren't sure, we would rather talk to strangers.

But think about it this way. If we had a great opportunity that helped people, wouldn't we want to offer it to people we know first? Why would we spend money advertising this great opportunity to strangers? If we felt like we were offering a chance to earn $10,000 a month, would we really run an ad looking for strangers?

Of course not. We need to rethink our commitment and belief in our business.

#2. We don't feel our friends and relatives will respect the offer because it came from us. Maybe we made mistakes in the past. Or, possibly all of our friends are rich and successful, while we are not. This can cause us to be shy and not contact them.

But there is a solution. All we do is offer them an "option" to hear about it or not. If everyone says "no" to the option of hearing our opportunity, no problem. We did our job. We gave them their chance. If they want to prejudge our opportunity based upon what happened to us in our past, that is their choice.

At least we won't have to worry about them coming to us later when we are successful and saying, "Why didn't you tell me about this earlier?"

THE SIX LEVELS OF COMMUNICATION.

We have to talk to our prospects, so why not talk at the highest level of communication? Why not give ourselves the best chance for success?

What happens when we don't communicate effectively? Think about this.

Almost everyone we talk to is pre-sold. They want our product or service. They want more money in their life. We have something most prospects want.

Yet, many prospects will tell us they aren't interested. Strange.

What goes wrong?

When we take the message inside our heads and try to put that message inside our prospects' heads ... something goes terribly, terribly wrong.

What our prospects understand is different from what we intended.

We want to start our business fast.

That means getting our message inside our prospects' heads as efficiently as possible. And by efficiently, we mean quickly and accurately.

Miscommunication slows this down. So we will always choose the highest level of communication possible when talking to our prospects. Let's take a look at these levels now.

Level One Communication
(talking <u>at</u> someone).

The lowest level of communication is a simple email or text message. Why? There are no visuals. We can't see our prospect's body language, and they can't see ours. And it gets worse.

- Our email could easily be misunderstood.

- It is a one-way communication. We are talking, but we don't get immediate feedback.

- It is harder to write correctly and clearly than when we talk to someone.

- And it is very impersonal. No one likes being treated like a lead or a statistic.

Now, a simple email or text message isn't bad, it is just the lowest form of communication. It is hard to communicate our belief, show our passion, and worst of all ... it can easily be deleted.

No sense of urgency, no appearance of importance, and just the bland written word makes this level of communication a difficult way to sell.

However, it may be our only means of communication. For instance, when we want to send out 30,000 copies of our newsletter, we know we don't have time to call everyone. Or sometimes we don't have our prospects' phone numbers. This might be the only way to get a message to them.

But here is where things really go wrong. Level One Communication is talking **at** someone. It is one-way communication.

There is no feedback. No nod of understanding or approval. We are blind to any reaction or questions from our prospects. It is just us, talking about us and what we have to offer. It isn't about our prospects. And that is boring to them.

In network marketing, our goal is to create relationships with people. The deeper the relationship, the stronger our group becomes. If we have low-level relationships with our team, our connections will be weak. This is not a strong base on which to build our business.

Think about dating. How strong would our relationships be if we only sent text messages? No pictures. Just one-way communication with text. We never meet in person. Not very effective, and not very enjoyable either.

Consider simple text messages as a low-level communication medium. We can do much better.

So whenever possible, let's try to communicate with our prospects at one of the higher levels.

Level Two Communication (talking <u>at</u> someone).

What is better than a simple text message?

A website. The company video. A brochure. At least we can include some graphics and some "talking head" videos.

Can we see the problem already? Yes. We are still talking **at** our prospects. One-way communication. We get no feedback, no approval, and no participation when we are talking **at** our prospects. We are still operating blind.

So we can pontificate, preach, and hype all we want, but maybe no one is reading or listening.

Feedback helps us make our message specific and targeted to our prospect. For instance, we want to write or talk about our company's background, but all our prospect is interested in is our product. This is not good communication. Good communication requires feedback.

All these "tools" slow our business down. They put off the decision to buy or join. We tell our prospects to spend time reviewing information. These actions delay the process:

- A video on our website. Our prospects don't have time to watch our video. They even hate watching a 15-second commercial. So when we send them to our website to watch a five-minute, 10-minute or 15-minute video, what will they think? They will think, "I don't have time to watch a 15-minute commercial. Let me quickly find a reason not to join." Now our prospects are looking for reasons not to join instead of looking for reasons to join. This is why we never see or hear from many prospects again.

- A brochure or detailed information pack. Again, we are talking **at** our prospects. And what is the most common result of giving out these information packs? Follow-up becomes difficult. If we do manage to re-connect with our prospects, they will most likely say, "I haven't had time to review it yet." That is a lot easier for them to tell us than to say they are not interested.

We might often hear this piece of advice, "Let the tools do the work."

This sounds good. We think, "All I have to do is get tools in hundreds of prospects' hands. Then my prospects will carefully evaluate the information and make an informed decision based upon the information presented." Just saying this out loud will give us a bad feeling. Why?

First, prospects don't have time to review information about our personal agenda. Already this feels like they are being sold to. Prospects don't like it.

Second, if getting tools and information into prospects' hands worked, then why would our network marketing companies need us? They could bypass us and simply get the information to prospects.

The reality is that it takes more than information and tools to build a relationship with our prospects. It takes us.

So why are there so many tools for distributors to use when tools are so ineffective?

Because new distributors who have poor or no network marketing communication skills. A tool with a low conversion rate is better than nothing. But this is why we want to graduate into real communication and relationship skills as quickly as possible. It is difficult to build a strong, long-term business by avoiding real conversations with people and simply passing out tools.

Level Three Communication (two-way communication).

Two-way communication?

Already this sounds better than talking **at** prospects.

A live telephone call with a prospect is two-way communication.

- We can give our prospect our message.
- We can listen for feedback.
- We can hear our prospect's tone of voice.
- We can check for understanding.
- We can answer our prospect's questions.
- We can hear our prospect sigh when we talk way too long. :)

We call this a ... conversation.

Now, we don't want to ruin this conversation by doing all the talking. Remember, this is two-way communication.

Having the chance to listen to our prospects, their concerns, and their interests helps us customize our presentation. Now we can talk about exactly what they want to know.

For example, we discover that this prospect doesn't want to know about the patent on our miracle product, but only wants to know if the company offers training. This makes our communication faster, more efficient, and more personal.

Our goal is to build our business fast. Two-way communication is much faster than simply sending a message.

Think of a typical messaging experience. We send the message, and wait for the reply. Then we send another short message, and wait for the reply. And then we... well, we know what happens. This can go on forever. With "live" two-way communication, we can shortcut this conversation. Five minutes of talking could replace five days of messaging.

Two-way communication allows us to move our prospects forward in the decision-making process. That's the direction we want to go ... forward.

Caution: Fatal mistake approaching.

Imagine we are engaging in Level Three Communication (two-way communication on a phone call) with a prospect.

Would we like to make the communication worse?

Would we like to handicap this conversation?

All we would have to do to make things worse is send our prospect to our ...

Website!

That is a lower level of communication. We took our conversation from a two-way communication (phone call) to a one-way communication, a website, which just talks **at** the prospect.

We went from a Level Three Communication down to a Level Two Communication!

We are going the wrong way.

And what happens when our prospects go to our website?

- They can't find the answer to a question they have.

- They get bored reading about the company's background.
- The video talks about something they are not interested in.
- They make a decision based on a one-minute glance.
- They look for a reason not to join or buy.
- They leave our page to check their social media.
- They miss the motivation from us to move forward.

Motivation from us?

Our products, services, and opportunity are great. We don't have to sell these. Our prospects already want better lives.

So what do we have to sell? Some hand-holding while our prospects make a change.

It is easy for our prospects to make a decision to buy or join. It is harder for them to implement this decision. Why? Because we all have programs in our minds that tell us, "Be careful. Don't change. We don't know what will happen in the future if we make a change." These programs often hold us back from better lives.

So our prospects want change, but they also don't want to make a mistake. They remember changes they made in the past that didn't work out. They want our hand-holding and confidence when they make their change to our products and opportunity. They want more support than just their personal decision.

Why? Because they know their friends will make fun of them if they make bad choices. And that is why we are here, to help them have the confidence to move forward.

We want to keep the conversation at the highest level possible, at least at Level Three Communication. Two-way communication gives our prospects the confidence to take action on their "yes" decision.

But what if we are brand-new distributors?

If we are new, we think, "I don't know what to say. I just want to pass out tools that talk **at** prospects. I don't even want to talk to anyone. Is there some way I can automate the process so I don't have to get involved?"

Well, we can think that, but isn't that taking a "victim mentality" instead of taking responsibility and learning exactly what to say?

To be professional, we will have to learn how to talk to people.

Let's do that now. Why?

Because here is the harsh reality about our prospects' decisions. Our friend, Kevin Graham, explained it best:

"When we learn exactly how our prospects make decisions, we understand that it is not the tool. It is what we say and do before the tool that will make the most difference. If we can't get our prospects to watch the video or join a presentation, our tool is useless."

Level Four Communication (two-way conversation via video).

While words are obviously critical, tonality and body language are equally as important. Non-verbal communication is huge.

Our words are important. Need proof? Say the wrong words and watch what happens.

But body language, facial expressions, and our tone of voice are also essential communication elements.

For example, with Level Four Communication, a video call, we can see our prospects' faces. We can see our prospects roll their eyes when we talk about the tiny details of our compensation plan. We can see our prospects fall asleep during our presentation.

But we can also see that slight smile when our prospects agree with us. That slight smile might tell us that we are talking about exactly what our prospects want to hear. We are communicating at a much higher level now.

With a video call, our prospects can see our faces and read our micro-facial expressions. Our prospects can gauge our interest in their part of the conversation.

It is easy to be rude when messaging, and easy to be rude to a faceless person over the phone. But it is a lot harder to be rude face-to-face on a video call. With face-to-face conversations, our prospects are much more polite.

How do we get reluctant prospects on a video call?

With better words, of course.

If our words are weak or uninspiring, our prospects make a "no" decision. They won't tell us "no" though. It is easier for them to save face by saying:

- "Please send me some information."

- "I will look at the website when I get a chance."

- "I will call you back when I have more time."

- "I am busy and traveling now, so send me the facts."

See a trend?

Weak words create "no" decisions. Prospects won't have the courage to make a change in their lives if our words are not compelling.

So what can we say to entice our prospects to have a higher level of communication with us? Here are some ideas.

1. Tell our prospects that we are offering one more option for their lives. This relieves their tension and fear of a high-pressure sales call.

2. Tell our prospects we have something to "demonstrate to them" that they can see via video. A simple, impressive product demonstration is an example of this technique.

3. Remind our prospects that we want to save them time. Tell our apprehensive prospects, "We can do this all in three minutes." With a one-minute presentation or two-minute story, this leaves us plenty of extra time for word pictures or chit-chat.

4. Tell our prospects, "You might want to see who you are dealing with. We are going to be partners for a long time." Then, make sure we smile. We don't want to look like a serial criminal.

If our prospects consistently resist video calls, we need to ask ourselves, "What did we say or do to cause this decision?" Yes, words are important.

There is a bonding when we see someone face-to-face. Let's use that bonding to communicate better.

Level Five Communication (two-way conversation in person).

What happens when we meet someone in person?

Now we have a different relationship and conversation than if we had just sent a text message. In person, there is a bonding that we can't get from a simple message. Think about this example.

Imagine that we know some fellow distributors from messages or phone calls. As we build more of a relationship, we look forward to meeting them in person. We participated together throughout the year in telephone conference calls and training. Now we look forward to meeting our distributor friends at the annual convention. There is a new, special bond created. We say, "Oh, I have been looking forward to meeting you in person all year!"

Humans are social.

That is why we are addicted to messaging, social media, and parties. We love to connect.

Connecting in person is so much more powerful than a text message or phone call.

Now consider this. If we could send a message to a prospect (Level One Communication), or meet the prospect face-to-face (Level Five Communication), which would we choose?

If we wanted to communicate at a higher level, be more effective, and save time, then yes, we would choose to meet in person.

We can see the tragedy approaching again.

Can we imagine meeting a prospect in person, having a two-way conversation, seeing the body language, listening to that person's concerns ... and then sending that prospect to a webpage?

Groan.

That is going from Level Five Communication, all the way down to Level Two Communication!

Now it makes sense when we hear professional network marketers say:

"The easiest way to get rid of prospects is to send them to a website."

This is funny only to those of us who know the six levels of communication.

We don't want to go down in our levels of communication. We want to go up. Here is an example.

We make contacts on social media. Initially they hesitate to communicate. Our goal is to move them up the communication ladder to a Level Three, Level Four, or even a Level Five conversation. When possible, we always want to improve our levels of communication.

This is not always possible. Here is an example.

We meet a great prospect on an airplane. This prospect lives 1,000 miles away. So even though we met this prospect in person at Level Five, it will be difficult to continue at this level.

We can't meet everyone in person. There are distance and time considerations. If we can't meet someone in person because they live thousands of miles away, simply choose the highest level of communication that is available to us.

For example, if we can't meet our prospects at Level Five, could we talk and see them at Level Four, a video phone call?

If not, could we talk to them at Level Three, a regular phone call?

Always choose the highest level of communication that is available to us.

Level Six Communication (two-way conversation in person, over food).

For centuries, people have bonded at banquets. There is a special connection when we meet someone in person over food.

The simple act of sharing a meal together guarantees a pleasant and polite two-way conversation. No one gets mad while having a meal with us.

Consider the quality, high-level communication of a simple business presentation over food. It may be more powerful than 1,000 messages or 10 ordinary phone conversations.

We are talking quality over quantity.

In network marketing, how many good quality people do we need to sponsor personally? Just a few. That is why we want to give ourselves the best chance with a high-quality, Level Six Communication "over a meal" experience.

We love meeting people over food. And if we talk too much, at least our prospect has a chance to say something while we chew our bites of food.

It is easy to meet people over food. We invite people to meet us over food every day. Simply say, "Hey, I know you are pressed for time, so let's meet over lunch. You have to eat anyway."

When having a conversation with prospects over food, tension goes away. This isn't a regular sales presentation. We communicate better when our prospects are relaxed and enjoying the food-filled bonding experience.

If we are new to network marketing, we might be thinking:

"But how do I show the company video and set up the flip-chart while we are eating?"

The reality is that our prospects make their final decision to do business with us before our presentation, not after. We will get our prospects' final decisions over the first minute or two of lunch with a one-minute presentation or a two-minute story.

Our prospects can see the supporting information later at their convenience. We will spend lunch talking about the big picture and what we want to do with our new business partnership.

People join people. They don't join companies or compensation plans. They don't have enough facts before they join. That comes later.

Since we only have to sponsor a few good people, our strategy could be:

"Just have a conversation with a different person every day for lunch and dinner ... until I find my few good people."

Gosh, that was easy.

This will take our focus away from expensive marketing, funnel advertising, capture pages, online videos, autoresponders, boring videos that no one will watch, etc.

Level Six Communication is having an enjoyable two-way communication with our prospects over food. It doesn't get any better than that.

Whenever possible, go for Level Six!

So let's review.

- **Level One Communication:** A simple message.
- **Level Two Communication:** A webpage, video, or brochure.

These are low-level, one-way communications that talk **at** prospects.

Having a conversation with someone is two-way communication. Now we can be effective.

- **Level Three Communication:** A phone call.
- **Level Four Communication:** A video call.
- **Level Five Communication:** Meeting someone in person.

- **Level Six Communication:** Meeting someone in person ... over food.

Always choose the highest level of communication that is available to us.

LEVEL SIX COMMUNICATION SOUNDS AWESOME, BUT ...

We may be thinking, "I am not full-time. I can't meet many people over food."

Let's make this work. Why?

Because Level Six Communication gives us the best chance to build a good relationship with our future leaders. How about an example?

Once a week, our friend Jerry Scribner spends most of his day at a Panera Bread Cafe. It is the perfect mobile office. Free wi-fi, unlimited refills on coffee, and the perfect place to meet with people.

If Jerry's prospects are early risers or on their way to work, they can meet him early for coffee or a quick breakfast.

Prospects get their questions answered. They meet and bond with Jerry. They think, "Jerry is a nice guy. I like his relaxed approach. He is someone I would love to do business with."

Now what happens when those prospects get back on the freeway and fight the traffic to their jobs? What are they thinking?

They might think, "If Jerry can do this business, so can I. Learning how to drink coffee and eat breakfast can't be all that hard. And having a nice chat with people a few times in the morning? I could do this too, and still keep my current job. And over time, like Jerry, I could quit my job and do this full-time. I bet he is leaving for the golf course now as he finishes his breakfast."

When Jerry doesn't have prospects sitting across the table from him, he catches up on busy work such as his emails and messages.

The restaurant staff starts asking what their happy customer is doing. Regular customers ask what he is doing. The flow of prospects never ends.

When Jerry gets bored, he goes to another restaurant for breakfast and meets a new group of prospects.

We don't have to be there all day.

We could have a Level Six breakfast meeting every day before we go to work. Or, why not do this for our lunch every day? We are surrounded by employees who want to look for alternatives to their day-to-day grind.

Every person drinks coffee or eats at least once a day. Do coffee drinkers feel comfortable drinking coffee? Do people feel comfortable eating lunch? Yes!

Now we are speaking to them at Level Six.

Pizza, anyone?

Set an entire Saturday aside to meet prospects over pizza. Meet them at a local pizza parlor, one or two prospects at a time. Continually order pizza all day while meeting with new prospects.

It won't sound scary to prospects to meet someone over a slice or two of pizza. Our two-minute story doesn't take long, and then we can talk about the details or partnering for the future.

The invitation? We could talk to someone during the week and say, "Let's meet for a slice or two of pizza on Saturday. How about 2pm? I know you have to pick up your son from practice at 3pm. This business may or may not be a good option for you now, but who knows what the future will bring? And we can catch up a bit too."

Okay, we can put together a much better invitation than that, but we get the point. It isn't hard to fill our Saturday with appointments if we are offering people one more option for their lives.

What about business presentations?

Renting a hotel meeting room can be expensive. Plus, when we invite guests to a hotel business opportunity meeting, sometimes they worry that a big sales pitch is coming. It is easier to invite these guests to a business dinner.

Are business dinners expensive? We might find that they are the same price or even less expensive than renting a hotel meeting room. Plus, our guests can come directly from their jobs and have an early dinner. They will be home much earlier than if they had to go to a business presentation that started later.

Many restaurants have banquet rooms. They are happy to allow us to use these banquet rooms for free, as long as we buy dinner. This is a win-win situation. The restaurant gets more business. Our guests get a free dinner. We will have more guests that want to come. And our costs are the same as an expensive hotel meeting room.

Bond with our group.

Here is Keith's strategy for Saturday trainings that help his group feel a strong connection with the company and the team.

After his local group became too big to fit into a coffee shop, he moved the monthly Saturday training to hotels. There was always a convenient lunch break in the middle of the day's workshop.

This was a perfect time for the team to bond over food. But there were a few issues.

- Some people wanted to bring their lunch.
- Other people wanted to go out to lunch.
- Some people wanted to eat at the hotel.
- Other people wanted to check out the local area.
- The hotel couldn't feed so many distributors during a short lunch break.
- The scheduled lunch break could turn into almost two hours.

Yikes!

Keith's solution?

Charge a few dollars extra for the Saturday training, and include lunch. Not the expensive full-service hotel lunch. Who wants to pay $50 for lunch? Instead, the group moved to "limited-service" hotels.

Many "limited service" hotels use their breakfast room during breakfast hours only. Then they lock the doors until the next morning.

His group rented the hotel meeting room, and then asked if they could use the empty breakfast room to set up their catered lunch. Keith always ordered extra to take care of the employees that worked at the hotel. The employees couldn't wait for Keith and the group to come back.

The group saved hundreds of dollars per Saturday meeting, but the real magic was with the team. They didn't get distracted by leaving during the lunch hour. The team communicated at Level Six for the entire lunch period. The family atmosphere of having a group lunch made team members come back again and again for training.

I love monthly banquets.

When I began my network marketing business in Chicago in 1972, it was a slow start. But as soon I had a few members on my local team, I organized a monthly banquet. I thought, "People go out for dinner at least once a month. Why not go out with their fellow team members?"

Everyone paid for their own dinner. This wasn't a big expense for me as a leader. My group had a chance to share experiences over the month, and rekindle their belief in our business. It is easier to believe when we surround ourselves with people with the same beliefs.

Was the monthly banquet a big hit? A chance of rain could keep team members away from an opportunity meeting. But for the banquet? They proved they could be at the banquet on time even in the worst snowstorms. People love bonding over food.

And what would happen if our team members brought a guest along to our fun group dinners? Yes, we could even use this activity to sponsor more new team members.

If we are going to build our business fast, not only do we have to enroll new people, but we also must keep the ones we have.

FOLLOW UP? UGH!

We know the old saying, "The fortune is in the follow-up."

But follow-up is boring. No one answers their phone. No one wants to return their messages. And if we do get a few prospects on the phone, they pretend to be rushed or handling an emergency. They hate talking to salesmen. What a waste of time.

Oh wait! We do the same thing to the salespeople in our lives.

What happens when we hear our phone ring? If we are not expecting the call, 9 out of 10 times we allow the call to go to voicemail.

Why? We have no idea why are they calling. We have no clue how long this conversation will take. So like a secret agent, we hide silently and wait to review the caller's message.

If we are interested, or feel safe returning the call, we start by saying, "I just missed your call, what's up?"

This helps us avoid small talk and idle chit-chat when we are short on time. We can avoid rude or pushy salespeople. And our prospects lead the same busy lives that we do.

The result? We invest time in following up, but almost no one will take our calls. Few prospects return our messages. Getting to talk with prospects again is difficult.

What is our level of communication when this happens?

Zero.

Any communication is better than zero.

We want to avoid boring phone calls that no one answers.

We feel bad when no one gets back to us.

This takes too much time for such a little reward. This isn't building our business fast enough.

So what could we do? Use Level One Communication, a simple text message. Our prospects always have their phones with them. And they check their social media messages too.

Many of us have a secret addiction to the message notification sound. A message means someone is thinking about us, something is new, or maybe this could be important.

Do they check their text messages? You bet.

Should we message our prospects and nag them into submission? Of course not. But here is a non-pushy text message we can send.

"I know you are not interested in my business, but can you do me a favor? If you hear about anybody wanting to earn some extra money before the holidays, could you please recommend me?"

Will our prospects feel pressured? No.

Are they happy that we respected their decision not to join? Absolutely. In fact, they might be thinking,

"Great! I walked on the other side of the street when I saw you. I hid in the bathroom when we attended the same party. And I am tired of pretending my messages are messed up and I never got anything from you. I missed talking to you, dear friend. Now I can feel safe being friends with you again."

So what happens when our prospects get this message?

1. They feel relieved that we are okay with their "no" decision.

2. They feel thrilled that they can visit with us again without another sales pitch and more pressure.

3. They might feel a little guilty about their "no" decision because we invested time with them. They feel a little bit obligated to find us someone who might have an interest. This is a chance for referrals.

4. They might think, "What do you mean I am not interested? I will join just to prove you wrong." This is a common response from red personalities.

5. We feel good because we delivered our main message past their mental resistance. We reminded them of our benefits.

6. We saved time. This message only took a few seconds to write and send. And by copying and pasting, we could do our entire month's follow-up in a few minutes.

7. We don't feel rejected. The only prospects we'll hear from will be those with referrals, and those that decided to join.

Will we get a lot of referrals?

Maybe, maybe not. But any referrals are better than no referrals. By repeating our main benefit, we made it easy for them to think of anyone that might qualify.

Will we get prospects who change their minds? Yes. And then we can upgrade the conversation to a higher level. We can have a conversation with them or meet them in person.

When we do this exercise at live workshops, many distributors report getting appointments before the workshop is over. Their prospects were just waiting for someone to get back to them. Here are some typical responses:

- "Thank you, I appreciate the offer." (Not the response we're looking for, but at least our message got through.)

- "I've been meaning to call you. Can we talk tomorrow after work?" (Instant appointment to sign up.)

- "Thanks for following up. I've been super busy but I am still interested." (I still like how this business sounds to me. But today is not a good day.)

- "When can we get together?" (You've already explained the business. The only reason to get together is to join.)

- "What are you doing tomorrow?" (Can't wait to join.)

- "How does lunch next week sound?" (Yeah, I should join. Let's do it.)

- "Wait, what? Let me take a second look." (Life got in my way. I should do this.)

When the workshop attendees share these positive responses, even the skeptical distributors start messaging.

The simple formula.

Part 1. "I know you are not interested."

Part 2. "Can you do me a favor?"

Part 3. Remind them of our benefit.

If we know our prospects well, it will be easy to create the main benefit from our previous conversations. And when our main benefit solves a problem in our prospects' lives, our message becomes more powerful.

Here are some examples of this message for our opportunity:

"I know you are not interested in my business, but can you do me a favor? If you know any of your friends hate commuting to work, and would rather work out of their homes, can you please recommend me?"

"I know you are not interested in my business, but could you do me a favor? If you hear of anyone who wants to fire their boss, can you give them my phone number?"

"I know you are not interested in my business right now. I understand. But, can you do me a favor? If you know anybody who wants to retire early, can you please tell them to contact me?"

"I know you are too busy with the children and work right now. But, could you do me a favor? If you know any moms who want to work out of their homes so they would have more time with their children, would you pass on my phone number?"

"I know you are not interested in my part-time business, but could you do me a favor? If you know of anyone who would like to pay for the holidays with cash instead of credit cards, could you let them know about me?"

"I know you are not interested in my part-time business, but could you do me a favor? If you know of anyone who would like to earn an extra $700 before the holidays, could you let me know?"

But what about customers?

Yes, this works well for our potential customers too. Here are a few examples.

"I know you are not interested in our diet program, but can you do me a favor? If you hear of anyone who wants to lose an extra ten pounds before the summer, could you give them my phone number?"

"I know you are not interested in our energy drink, but can you do me a favor? If you see any of your co-workers yawning and struggling to stay awake in the afternoons, could you let them know I have a solution?"

"I know you are not interested in our anti-aging skincare line, but can you do me a favor? If you hear anybody complaining about looking old, could you refer them to my video?"

"I know you are not interested in our wrinkle cream, but can you do me a favor? If you hear anyone complain about their wrinkles, could you give them my phone number?"

"I know you are not interested in changing your electric service right now, but can you do me a favor? If you hear anyone complaining about their high electricity bill, can you please recommend me to them?"

"I know you are not interested in our shopping program, but can you do me a favor? If you know anyone who likes to pay lower prices instead of higher prices, can you please recommend me?"

"I know you are not interested in our travel club, but can you do me a favor? If you know anyone who wants to save up to 50% on their annual family holiday, can you please recommend me?"

"I know you are not interested in our legal service, but can you do me a favor? If you hear about anybody who likes to speed but doesn't like the speeding tickets, can you please recommend me?"

Easy, fast, and no rejection.

We can follow up with our entire list in minutes. For many of our prospects who are "thinking it over," we can cut and paste the same message and quickly send the text.

No rejection. We only hear from our prospects who want to take action. They might reply, "Hey, I am still interested. Just been too busy to get back to you."

If they are not interested, we don't hear back. And, some of our uninterested prospects might give us some referrals.

What about our new team members?

We might be saying to ourselves, "But my team members are not doing anything!"

When new distributors join, how many professional network marketing skills do they have? Zero.

What do new distributors have? A desire to build a business ... and a whole lot of issues and problems.

And then we complain, "My new distributors aren't doing anything!"

Instead of complaining, we need to help them get started. We should ask ourselves if we provided them with at least a few tiny skills or mindsets. For example:

- Did we write down, word-for-word, exactly what to say to their prospects over the phone? Or did we say, "Oh, I don't know exactly what to say. They are your friends. Do your best."

- Did we take away the fear of selling in their minds? Their fear of rejection? Did we give them the words to say to prevent negative feedback from their prospects?

- Did we write down, word-for-word, exactly what to say to their prospects to overcome the price objection?

- Did we write down, word-for-word, exactly what to say to get new prospects immediately?

- Did we write down, word-for-word, exactly what to say to the most common objections they would face?

We must do our part first. We have to give our new team members at least the minimum skills they will need when they start.

Our new team members already have motivation. They joined. Now it is our responsibility to give them skills so that they can go to work on their business.

If we do our part by giving motivated team members some great starting skills, they will surprise us with their business progress.

THIS ALL HAPPENS SO FAST.

Yes, we don't need a long, boring sales presentation to get people to say "yes" to what we offer. The human mind doesn't work like that.

Humans make decisions first. Then if the answer is "yes," we will want more information.

Huh?

If you haven't read the book, *Pre-Closing for Network Marketing*, here is a short overview of the decision-making process.

Ask a friend, "How do you make your decisions? Are they emotional? Do you tally up the number of reasons why versus the number of reasons why not? Is it some sort of hormonal thing? Little voices talking in your ear?"

Our friend's answer? "I don't know."

Well, we are in the decision-making business. That is our job. We must get our prospects to make a decision to buy our products or services, or to join our business.

Now, even if our prospects don't know how they make decisions, what if we knew? Would this help us grow our business faster? Of course.

Let's ask ourselves, "Do we really know how our prospects make their final decisions?"

If we have only just started in network marketing, we won't know. This isn't taught in school.

But brain science makes this question easy to answer. Without getting technical, here is a short guide that will help us understand how our prospects make their decisions.

Our prospects have five "trigger" questions. These questions must be in the right order. If we could answer these questions in the right order, our prospects would feel relaxed when making decisions with us.

Here are the five "trigger" questions our prospects have.

Question #1. "Who are you?"

This is their survival program, hard at work. Everyone wants to survive. Now, would our prospects view us differently than a famous movie star? Of course. There would also be a difference if they already respected us, or if we ran over their pet on the way to visit them. Prospects judge harshly.

We can't change who we are in seconds. This will take time. This is the reason for personal development. As we accumulate better internal programs and attitudes, we gain respect in the eyes of our prospects.

Question #2. "Can I trust you and believe you?"

This is the biggest question in our prospects' minds. No matter how good our opportunity or products may be, if our prospects don't believe us, we are dead.

We have a few critical seconds to establish this trust and belief. Amateurs waste these first few seconds. Professionals? Well, they know exactly how to manage these seconds. If we get this right, the rest of the steps are easy.

If we have good rapport skills, our careers will be almost effortless.

Question #3. "Are you interesting?"

There are thousands of pieces of data competing for our prospects' attention. We have to rise above these competing inputs. Remember that short attention span of humans?

If we are not interesting, our prospects' minds will drift away and we will lose them.

Humans don't want to listen to details about something they have no interest in. We have to be interesting first. Then they will want to hear more details.

Question #4. "Do I want to do it, or not?"

Brain science has established that our prospects' final decisions happen in the first few seconds. This is great news for us. If we get our prospect's final decision within the first 10 or 15 seconds, then our prospect will be on our side for the rest of our conversation.

It seems strange that closing happens before our prospects know anything about our offer. New skills like this will propel us to faster growth.

Question #5. "Can you give me the details?"

Yes, decisions happen w-a-a-ay before our presentation even begins. We only give presentations to prospects who make the "yes" decision first.

Amateurs believe the final decision happens after the presentation. Professionals know the final decision happens before the presentation.

But now that our prospects have decided that we are interesting and that this is something they want to do, now they are willing to hear the details. This is where we give our presentation.

Some prospects want a long presentation with a lot of details. Others don't want any details. They are ready to take action now.

CAN WE IMPROVE?

Of course. This quick start guide is only the beginning.

We want to learn the four core skills as soon as possible. Every time we meet a "live" prospect, we will use these four basic skills:

1. Rapport.

2. Ice breakers.

3. Closing.

4. Presentation.

But we don't have to wait. We can start now.

We can build our network marketing business and earn bonuses while we learn these four core skills.

But our potential is much, much greater. We will want to learn skills such as:

- The four color personalities.
- Word pictures.
- Follow-up.
- Needs versus wants.
- Subconscious mind programs.
- Magic word sequences.
- Great first sentences.

- Sound bites.

- Prospecting skills.

- Leadership skills.

- And many, many more.

As we learn more skills, we become more attractive to our prospects. They want us to be their guide to success.

Plus, with better skills, we get better results.

Don't wait. Start now.

Here is our chance to grow fast in our new and exciting career.

THANK YOU.

Thank you for purchasing and reading this book. We hope you found some ideas that will work for you.

Before you go, would it be okay if we asked a small favor? Would you take just one minute and leave a sentence or two reviewing this book online? Your review can help others choose what they will read next. It would be greatly appreciated by many fellow readers.

I travel the world 240+ days each year.
Let me know if you want me to stop in your
area and conduct a live Big Al training.

→ **BigAlSeminars.com** ←

FREE Big Al Training Audios

Magic Words for Prospecting

plus Free eBook and the Big Al Report!

→ **BigAlBooks.com/free** ←

MORE BIG AL BOOKS

BIGALBOOKS.COM

The Two-Minute Story for Network Marketing
Create the Big-Picture Story That Sticks!

Worried about presenting your business opportunity to prospects? Here is the solution. The two-minute story is the ultimate presentation to network marketing prospects.

How to Build Your Network Marketing Business in 15 Minutes a Day

Anyone can set aside 15 minutes a day to start building their financial freedom. Of course we would like to have more time, but in just 15 minutes we can change our lives forever.

How to Meet New People Guidebook
Overcome Fear and Connect Now

Meeting new people is easy when we can read their minds. Discover how strangers automatically size us up in seconds, using three basic standards.

Why Are My Goals Not Working?
Color Personalities for Network Marketing Success

Setting goals that work for us is easy when we have guidelines and a checklist.

Closing for Network Marketing
Getting Prospects Across The Finish Line

Here are 46 years' worth of our best closes. All of these closes are kind and comfortable for prospects, and rejection-free for us.

Pre-Closing for Network Marketing
"Yes" Decisions Before The Presentation

Instead of selling to customers with facts, features and benefits, let's talk to prospects in a way they like. We can now get that "yes" decision first, so the rest of our presentation will be easy.

The One-Minute Presentation
Explain Your Network Marketing Business Like A Pro

Learn to make your business grow with this efficient, focused business presentation technique.

Retail Sales for Network Marketers
How to Get New Customers for Your MLM Business

Learn how to position your retail sales so people are happy to buy. Don't know where to find customers for your products and services? Learn how to market to people who want what you offer.

Getting "Yes" Decisions
What insurance agents and financial advisors can say to clients

In the new world of instant decisions, we need to master the words and phrases to successfully move our potential clients to lifelong clients. Easy … when we can read their minds and service their needs immediately.

3 Easy Habits For Network Marketing
Automate Your MLM Success

Use these habits to create a powerful stream of activity in your network marketing business.

Start SuperNetworking!
5 Simple Steps to Creating Your Own Personal Networking Group

Start your own personal networking group and have new, pre-sold customers and prospects come to you.

The Four Color Personalities for MLM
The Secret Language for Network Marketing
Learn the skill to quickly recognize the four personalities and how to use magic words to translate your message.

Ice Breakers!
How To Get Any Prospect To Beg You For A Presentation
Create unlimited Ice Breakers on-demand. Your distributors will no longer be afraid of prospecting, instead, they will love prospecting.

How To Get Instant Trust, Belief, Influence and Rapport!
13 Ways To Create Open Minds By Talking To The Subconscious Mind
Learn how the pros get instant rapport and cooperation with even the coldest prospects. The #1 skill every new distributor needs.

First Sentences for Network Marketing
How To Quickly Get Prospects On Your Side
Attract more prospects and give more presentations with great first sentences that work.

Motivation. Action. Results.
How Network Marketing Leaders Move Their Teams
Learn the motivational values and triggers our team members have, and learn to use them wisely. By balancing internal motivation and external motivation methods, we can be more effective motivators.

How To Build Network Marketing Leaders
Volume One: Step-By-Step Creation Of MLM Professionals
This book will give you the step-by-step activities to actually create leaders.

How To Build Network Marketing Leaders

Volume Two: Activities And Lessons For MLM Leaders

You will find many ways to change people's viewpoints, to change their beliefs, and to reprogram their actions.

The Complete Three-Book Network Marketing Leadership Series

Series includes: How To Build Network Marketing Leaders Volume One, How To Build Network Marketing Leaders Volume Two, and Motivation. Action. Results.

51 Ways and Places to Sponsor New Distributors

Discover Hot Prospects For Your Network Marketing Business

Learn the best places to find motivated people to build your team and your customer base.

How to Follow Up With Your Network Marketing Prospects

Turn Not Now Into Right Now!

Use the techniques in this book to move your prospects forward from "Not Now" to "Right Now!"

How To Prospect, Sell And Build Your Network Marketing Business With Stories

If you want to communicate effectively, add your stories to deliver your message.

26 Instant Marketing Ideas To Build Your Network Marketing Business

176 pages of amazing marketing lessons and case studies to get more prospects for your business immediately.

Big Al's MLM Sponsoring Magic

How To Build A Network Marketing Team Quickly

This book shows the beginner exactly what to do, exactly what to say, and does it through the eyes of a brand-new distributor.

Public Speaking Magic

Success and Confidence in the First 20 Seconds

By using any of the three major openings in this book, we can confidently start our speeches and presentations without fear.

Worthless Sponsor Jokes

Network Marketing Humor

Here is a collection of worthless sponsor jokes from 25 years of the "Big Al Report." Network marketing can be enjoyable, and we can have fun making jokes along the way.

How To Get Kids To Say Yes!

Using the Secret Four Color Languages to Get Kids to Listen

Turn discipline and frustration into instant cooperation. Kids love to say "yes" when they hear their own color-coded language.

ABOUT THE AUTHORS

Keith Schreiter has 20+ years of experience in network marketing and MLM. He shows network marketers how to use simple systems to build a stable and growing business.

So, do you need more prospects? Do you need your prospects to commit instead of stalling? Want to know how to engage and keep your group active? If these are the types of skills you would like to master, you will enjoy his "how-to" style.

Keith speaks and trains in the U.S., Canada, and Europe.

Tom **"Big Al" Schreiter** has 40+ years of experience in network marketing and MLM. As the author of the original "Big Al" training books in the late '70s, he has continued to speak in over 80 countries on using the exact words and phrases to get prospects to open up their minds and say "YES."

His passion is marketing ideas, marketing campaigns, and how to speak to the subconscious mind in simplified, practical ways. He is always looking for case studies of incredible marketing campaigns that give usable lessons.

As the author of numerous audio trainings, Tom is a favorite speaker at company conventions and regional events.

Made in the
USA
Monee, IL